T0132212

FLIGHT

to the

MOUNTAIN TOP

Pablo Marquez-Garcia

AuthorHouse™
1663 Liberty Drive
Bloomington, IN 47403
www.authorhouse.com
Phone: 833-262-8899

This book is printed on acid-free paper.

ISBN: 979-8-8230-1045-0 (sc)
ISBN: 979-8-8230-1046-7 (e)

Print information available on the last page.

Published by AuthorHouse 06/16/2023

authorHOUSE®

CONTENTS

. . . .

ABOUT THE AUTHOR

Pablo Marquez grew up in various places around the world. As a child his activities included hiking, swimming, biking, football, baseball, basketball, reading and guitar playing. He attended Pedro A. Campos High School and Friends University. With a BS in HR Management Degree he has worked primarily in the logistics field receiving his Global Supply Chain Mgmt Certification and has traveled extensively to various countries to implement Materials and Purchasing departments and speaks fluent Spanish and English along with conversational German. His first novel Benito's Treasure Hunt, was written as a remembrance to his various childhood experiences while growing up and in sharing them with his children. Recently, he has published three other Kids novels; <u>Flight To The Mountain Top</u>, <u>Cruise' in</u> and <u>Max - A Life of a Tree</u>. <u>Flight To The Mountain Top</u>, reflecting on how even a day out in a child's life can lead to experiences that are life-long remembrances. While <u>Cruise' in</u>, narrates how a defunct vacation trip can turn certain incidents into real life satisfaction along with the help of friends. And finally <u>Max - A Life of a Tree,</u> Is an earlier in life story of Max and his Grand Father and their many ways trees can help us. Soon to be released is <u>Costume</u>, a riveting account of how life seems to complicate itself when all in the game work against each other. This Novel will be released in 2022, for Ages 15 and above.

PREFACE

To fulfill another childhood story, P. Marquez-Garcia, he again has written within a family story with a great setting and tasteful writing. A ban of close school kids setting out to achieve goals and sharing as friends. As it had to be they run into life and death situations that make you think that they have had it. This short story novel is available in ebook format great for 5-15 years old to read.

ABOUT THE BOOK

In our early lifetime there were not many Arcades, Fun Centers or Mini Golfs' so you had to make your own fun and adventure. There were times in which Pablo, his Brother and our friends would be building a make believe camp or fort sometimes it was so interesting to build that we would forget about lunch and play all day long. We would eat cherries and pears from the neighborhood trees and loved every minute we spent as friends and family. Pablo and his brother were active in Football, Baseball and Basketball. They were lucky to have nature so close that they would hike in a days time 10-12 miles and not quiver about it. <u>Flight To The Mountain Top</u> was one such of story living in Germany and Hans was a German boy our age and we would find friendships that we cherish even today. Today we still love walking the Trails throughout Florida.

CHAPTER 1

WAKING UP

As Manuel and Emilio woke up early that Saturday morning, they knew exactly what they were going to do. They've only been talking about it for sometime now; and even falling asleep at night would keep them up for several hours before they would fall asleep mumbling their last words over the great adventures. "We'll have lots of fun!" and a last sigh they were both fast asleep. Looking out the window Manuel noticed that during the night a thin sheet of snow had fallen and made the small mountain behind their home look majestic and adventurous.

CHAPTER 2

. . . .

HIKING TOWARDS THE MOUNTAIN

Manuel, Emilio and Hans, "Let's go down this dirt road that'll lead us to the mountain road?" Up ahead the road turned towards the forest again. "Let's cut through here", said Hans, then we'll be heading directly towards the mountain top! The creek was frozen solid. Emilio yelled "look it's frozen over! Let's slide over it." Manuel put one foot on the ice and Emilio yelled, "Watch out! It can be thin ice and you'll fall right through, so be careful!"

CHAPTER 3

SCALING THE MOUNTAIN

Having arrived at record time the boys sat looking and pointing where they lived and where they would have to route back when suddenly they heard loud galloping. The sound was coming in their directions. Hans looked up towards the peak and noticed some Elk strutting downward towards the base of the mountain. They were headed exactly for the moss for their noontime grazing. They sat in silence as they saw the leader, tall and bountiful; with a full head gear of horns and the rest of the herd following close behind him. They passed next to the boys as if they did not exist.

CHAPTER 4

WATERY GRAVE

Hans found that the creek was wider than where they first crossed but soon found a solid place where they could cross over. Hans had no time to pause, daring as always he threw himself on the ice. "Whee, Whee! This is fun! Come on guys!" exclaimed Hans. It took just a few moments of hesitation before Manuel would join Hans. The question was, "who would slide the furthest?"

CHAPTER 5

....

HEADING HOME

Manuel slid and fell up ahead, while Emilio and Hans looked on from a distance. "Are you all right?" asked Emilio. "I'm fine, as he giggled getting up again to continue the bet of who would slide the furthest." Here I go! As Manuel ran a few feet he jumped into the air and when landing, suddenly both feet dug deep into the ice. "Hey you guys I'm stuck, come get me out!" yelled Manuel. Emilio and Hans looked over towards Manuel; they saw him sinking like an anchor into the water. "Help!" yelled Manuel. As Hans turned to run towards the last place they saw Manuel they heard a faint sound and murmuring. Emilio and Hans were surprised. "What is it, what is it saying? " asked Hans. Near the bank of the creek! "Emilio couldn't believe his eyes! The murmuring sound was coming from along the bank all right! Manuel's Hand stuck out of the bank. He was waving it through a small hole in the ice.

Emilio wrapped the blanket around Manuel. "You boys from the neighborhood?" asked Mrs. Mueller. "Yes, we were here last summer getting minnows and plants for school" answered Emilio. They walked rapidly towards the Mueller's home where they sat next to the chimney fire and drank warm chocolate.

THE END

Other Pablo Marquez-Garcia Kids Novels

Also Sold On Authorhouse, NOOK, Barnes & Noble websites

<u>Benito's Treasure Hunt</u>,

<u>Max - A Life of a Tree 2019</u>

<u>Cruse'in 2002</u>

<u>Pablo Marquez-Garcia</u>

Would you like to write to the Author? I will let you know when the next Raffle will be held.

P.O.Box 1051

Bell, FL 32619

Copyright ™

Printed in the United States
by Baker & Taylor Publisher Services